The
Dragonfly
in the
Haze

Also in the **be̲i̲ng human** series:

The Lost Sun

The Flower in the Pocket

The Unwanted Friend

For more information about the Being Human method, please refer
to each book in the series. You will also find a video overview of
the method via www.carriehayward.com/beinghuman. Further,
you will find more information about the teachings in the list
of resources provided at the end of this book.

The Dragonfly in the Haze

A **being human** guide to
creating meaningful connection

DR CARRIE HAYWARD

Illustrated by Elizabeth Szekely

Dr Carrie Hayward is a clinical psychologist who works with individuals to help them live more consciously and purposefully. Her training in Acceptance and Commitment Therapy (ACT) profoundly changed her approach to living, both professionally and personally.

First published 2023

Exisle Publishing Pty Ltd
PO Box 864, Chatswood, NSW 2057, Australia
226 High Street, Dunedin, 9016, New Zealand
www.exislepublishing.com

A CiP record for this book is available from the National Library of Australia.

ISBN 978-1-922539-91-5

Designed by Bee Creative
Typeset in Optima, 10.5pt
Printed in China

This book uses paper sourced under ISO 14001 guidelines from well-managed forests and other controlled sources.

10 9 8 7 6 5 4 3 2 1

Disclaimer

While this book is intended as a general information resource and all care has been taken in compiling the contents, neither the author nor the publisher and their distributors can be held responsible for any loss, claim or action that may arise from reliance on the information contained in this book. As each person and situation is unique, it is the responsibility of the reader to consult a qualified professional regarding their personal care.

Introduction

"

How rare and beautiful it truly is, that we exist.

—'Saturn', Sleeping At Last

Being human is truly remarkable. Our mere existence is beautiful, wondrous and mindbogglingly mysterious. But when it comes to the everyday and ordinary experience of being human, at times it can be really hard.

My years as a psychologist have taught me why — that is, the core reason as to why human beings are prone to psychological struggle. I believe this is one of the most important understandings I have learnt about the human condition.

You see, people come to see me, or any psychologist, with a vast range of struggles. Some of us struggle with depressive states or anxiety issues. For others, it may be anger concerns, eating issues, or disharmony in our relationships, and so on. And these experiences are occurring on the background of our own histories and contexts.

It is therefore easy to forget that we are all from the same species, existing together on planet Earth — all trying to navigate life the best way we can. Given our internal world feels deeply private and isolated, we often assume that our psychology is different or abnormal — that there is something wrong with us — which can make us feel alone. Like we do not belong.

Yet despite our differences, all human beings share one of the greatest dilemmas of the human condition: our innate struggle with all the things we cannot control in our lives, including the hardships that happen around us and the emotional pain that happens inside us. And this is underpinned by a core function of our humanness: our survival response. This remarkable aspect of the human condition that keeps us alive can, paradoxically, work against us when we are experiencing hardship and pain. Our hardwired need for control can typically result in a disconnect with ourselves and our core values, which disrupts our way of being with ourselves, each other and the world. And it is when we are disconnected from our values — how we want to show up in the world — that we experience the greatest distress.

In short, our psychological struggle fundamentally occurs when our *humanness* disrupts our *beingness*.

I wrote the Being Human series to explore this dilemma of the human condition. The series is informed by Acceptance and Commitment Therapy (ACT) teachings, an evidence-based framework which helps us to develop psychological flexibility in order to live a mindful, values-based and purposeful life. Put simply, the essence of practising ACT is bringing awareness, and acceptance, to the 'human' in our experience, which allows us to bring choice and meaning to the 'being' in our moments. Allowing us to live our moments, and therefore our lives, as conscious and connected human beings.

"

All life is linked to the earth from which it came.

—Rachel Carson, The Sense of Wonder

The Being Human series features four stories that follow the journey of interconnected characters, illuminating the different ways we experience our shared struggle of the human condition. The stories are followed by an exploration into the teaching and conclude with a practical process for you to take into your life. Each book focuses on a different teaching, and therefore can stand alone, where you will learn one helpful process at a time.

This book in your hands — *The Dragonfly in the Haze* — focuses on our increasing disconnection with the physical world, including our growing disconnect with each other, and how this disconnect is impacting our meaning and vitality in life. Through this story, you will learn about how we can consciously reconnect to our surroundings, in each present moment, including reigniting our sense of wonder about each other and the world.

Each book is one piece of the Being Human puzzle. The whole series — all books connected — forms the complete Being Human method.

By reading about the story of the characters in each book, you may see some of your own experience in their challenges. And hopefully, you will discover the power of awareness around your humanness, allowing you to engage with your values and have choice over your beingness, with yourself, others and the world. This is at the heart of our purpose and meaning as human beings.

And so, welcome aboard to Being Human. I hope you have an insightful and wondrous ride.

x Carrie

The story

It's his last life. Walter reaches the edge of the dense forest. A raspy caw of a crow and the rustle of trees resound in the distance. He races towards the giant-sized ornamental door, as grenades, darting out from behind the trees, threaten to shoot him down. And seemingly out of nowhere, a giant green dragon-like insect with razor-sharp teeth and dominating eyes soars in. Walter tries to sneak underneath the arc of its wide-stretched wings. But it's no good. The mythical creature captures Walter in one gulp.

Game over. Walter throws down the game console, which crashes with unsatisfying silence on the carpeted floor.

Walter looks at the clock on the wall. Midday.

How did it get to be lunchtime already? He sighs.

Surely the phone call will come today, he hopes, with a shade of desperation.

As he slumps back into the soft couch, Walter notices a grey haze hovering within the living room. He looks out through the window to find a blackened sky and then looks back around him — it's as though the darkness has seeped inside.

As Walter sluggishly leans forward to pick up the game console, his other arm reaches up to the wall behind him —

muscle memory guides his hand towards the light switch. But the lights do not come on. He barely notices as a vibration from the coffee table interrupts him. Walter's heart leaps. He reaches over eagerly to pick up his phone.

'See you this afternoon Walt!' the text reads, next to an animated icon of a face with scant resemblance to his best friend. His heart slumps. He ignores the message and sidetracks to the next notification instead. Walter is taken to a heated conversation — hundreds of people chirping their opinion about the latest controversy surrounding his favourite basketballer.

Continuing to scrawl through the tweets, he finds himself on another post deep down the virtual rabbit hole. Booming music coming from the large screen then alerts Walter, beckoning him to come back to land with the foreboding giant insect.

He pauses. *I should probably go for a run instead.*

The lights suddenly flicker above him. His eyes search around him, eagerly looking for any reason to keep him here. They land back on the gloomy sky.

It can wait until after I get the call, he convinces himself, just as a low rumble radiates from his stomach.

He presses pause on the game and his hunger drags his body out through the living room door.

Walter scuffles down the hallway towards the kitchen, head down while scrolling through the news headlines. He bangs his knee into the pantry cupboard. *Argh*, he winces, giving it a vigorous rub with his free hand.

He opens the pantry door. He stares blankly. He can't decide. Walter shuts the pantry door and opts for a banana from the fruit bowl on the kitchen bench.

He leans against the bench and opens his online calendar. Walter counts the days. It has now been seven days of waiting. He fantasizes about the phone ringing and hearing good news. A jolt of aliveness within his chest accompanies this vision, like a sparked flame reminding him, tantalizing him, about what it used to feel like before the gruelling waiting began. But it's a fleeting flame without enough gas to stay ignited. A sense of fatigue resumes.

Walter peels the banana and throws the skin into the rubbish bin under the sink. He sees the high stack of dishes filling the sink, now caked with dried crumbs. *They can wait until after.*

Walter takes a bite of the banana. It tastes bland.

It must be unripe, he assumes.

He turns back to his calendar and sees the notification for the party today. His best friend's message springs back to mind. Walter sighs.

I suppose I had better go, he reluctantly concedes.

He looks around for his blue cap and spots it in the corner of the bench next to his wallet. Rather, it's what he thought was his blue cap. Walter picks it up and turns it in his hands. It's now an icy grey colour instead.

It must have faded in the wash, he supposes.

He shrugs and slaps it on his head, picks up his wallet and heads back down the hallway and out the front door into the hazy outside air. He reaches into his pockets for his earbuds, pops them into his ears and taps into his podcast library. His mind then takes him to thinking about the search results he found on his phone yesterday — mixed results that have had him jumping from hopefulness to worst-case scenario ever since.

Back and forth like a swinging pendulum clock. Walter notices that the sound in his ears is very quiet. He presses the 'up' button on the side of his phone. But the volume bar is already at its maximum.

There must be something wrong with my earbuds, he concludes.

He flips to his messages again, just in case. Nothing is there. His stomach churns. As he tries checking his missed call list instead, his face is suddenly tickled by a bushy branch of jasmine hanging over the footpath. He whips the branch out of his eyes. Despite it being so close, he can't smell the usually fragrant shrub.

It must have lost its smell, he decides.

Walter arrives at the bus shelter at the end of the street. He plonks down on the worn-out timber bench, and taps into his favourite word game. A message pops up from the game's bot.

'Where have you been my friend? I have missed you.'

'Sorry, I'm back!' Walter quickly texts to the bot, while he begins to mentally calculate his next move.

Minutes pass before the outside air tickles

Walter's nose, causing him to sneeze three times. It jolts him alert, and he looks up. He sees the back of the bus. It's shrouded by the haze, riddled with smoky fumes billowing out of its exhaust pipe. And it's driving away. He shakes his head in astonishment.

How on earth did I miss that?

Walter looks at the time on his phone. He is now going to miss half of the party.

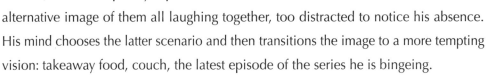

He pictures the faces of friends looking around for him, and then quickly replaces this with an alternative image of them all laughing together, too distracted to notice his absence. His mind chooses the latter scenario and then transitions the image to a more tempting vision: takeaway food, couch, the latest episode of the series he is bingeing.

Walter stands up and begins to head back home.

The next morning Walter wakes up and grimaces. There is a pain in the right side of his neck. He is on the couch, fully clothed. A half-eaten pizza is still sitting on the coffee table.

Walter looks around him. The haze inside has thickened further. It feels very dark. His eyes land on his laptop sitting on the coffee table.

I should really do some study, he considers, waiting for his body to kick into gear. But all he feels is a flat mood idling in his head and leaking down into his torso. Refusing to comply.

He yawns in a deep, drawn out way and sinks further into the cushions of the couch.

I'll get back to it as soon as this is all over.

He checks the screen of his phone sitting next to him. Nothing. His stomach stirs; an uneasy sensation sloshes deep in the pit. He then leans over to pick up the game console.

Walter begins the formidable quest again. His stomach starts to settle as he makes his way across the vast openness of lifelike fields, eliciting a sense of freedom. He's racing with urgency, with the background of the familiar sounds of crows cawing and the swishing of trees in the simulated breeze. As he gets closer to the gigantic doors, more threatening sounds start to crescendo: he hears thunder grumbles in the sky, and menacing squeals of the giant flying insect coming towards him. And the incongruous sound of a melodic jingle …

Ah it's my phone!

Walter throws aside the console. This time it crashes loudly onto the hard timber coffee table. He quickly picks up his phone.

'Hello,' he chokes out.

'Walt, you're fine. The test results are all clear.'

The doctor's voice continues speaking, but Walter is barely listening. Shock has settled in.

'Thank you,' he whispers, before hanging up the phone. He is staring into space, digesting the news. It is what he has been waiting for. Shock slowly morphs into a feeling of warmth that glides around his stomach. Relief, followed by a surge of energy in his chest, as though his heart muscles are jigging for joy. He jumps up and heads for the shower, his feet springing down the hallway.

Walter finishes his shower and then walks to his bedroom to get dressed for the day. As he puts his trainers on, he notices something start to shift in his body. His hands, tying his laces, begin to slow down. He then suddenly stops.

What am I getting dressed for? he questions.

Walter thinks about the day ahead and all that he needs to do: *study, cleaning up, get back to exercise.*

A typical day. A very ordinary day.

He can feel the energy in his body begin to drop, like the hammer bell game at a carnival, where after ringing the bell, the puck flings back down just as quickly as it went up. This is not what he had expected to feel. It is not what he had been waiting for. He shifts his attention back to the earlier phone call, trying to re-ignite the elation of that first moment of hearing the news. Instead, his mind does the opposite, and starts to question …

But what if … they're not certain?

Walter pushes the thought away and finishes tying his laces. He begins to walk out of his bedroom just as his phone pings. It's a message from his mother:

'Don't forget about tomorrow and please don't be late, x.'

Urgh. I had forgotten about tomorrow. Walter deletes the message and taps back into his word game. At the same time, he wanders aimlessly around the house. The haze is still hovering inside. He ends up back in the living room and slumps onto the couch. His eyes land on the big screen, offering a different world. And one that promises to swallow all unwanted feelings.

Hours pass. Walter is now back to watching his series. Although he is hardly watching, barely managing to expel a mediocre laugh when the TV audience does. The closing

13

credits roll and the next episode is about to start. He hasn't moved for hours; his legs are weighted, his eyes have dimmed, and his chest flattens with each episode.

Snap out of it! a voice inside of him bites. But it is faint.

His pocket beeps, which shifts his attention. He picks up his phone to find a message from his best friend:

'We're outside your gate. You're coming to kick the football with us.'

Walter sighs. He tries to think of a reason, any reason, to avoid going. He contemplates ignoring the message, pretending he's not home. But he feels too fatigued to fight it. Walter concedes and slowly makes his way to the front door, picking up his cap and a small tin of mints from the hallway table on the way. He opens his front door to find his two best friends, one carrying a green football under his arm, on the other side of the timber picket fence. Walter attempts a half smile.

'How's this haze?' he offers as he walks through the gate. His two friends look at him with confusion. They both appear to ignore the comment and give Walter a fist punch.

They begin walking along the footpath, speckled with rain puddles from a previous downpour. They turn around the corner towards the local park. Walter's friends are deep in conversation about the party the day before. Their voices feel distant and muffled, as though they are speaking underwater. Walter is struggling to keep up as his mind takes him back to the phone call that morning. He continues to replay the words, desperately hoping that each re-run will make him feel better. But instead, the memory is fading, as though it's worn out from overuse.

They finally reach the park and head towards a large, grassed area just inside the entrance. The three friends spread out and begin kicking the football to one another.

'Walter! Earth to Walter!'

Walter is zoned out on the opposite side of the grassed patch to his friends. He jolts his head up, his eyes looking puzzled.

'The ball! Go and get it!' His friends point towards the hedged fence behind Walter.

Oh right. He comes back to the moment.

Walter holds one thumb up in acknowledgment, pretending he knows exactly where the ball has gone. He turns around and looks at the thick hedge. He begins to take off his shoes, expecting to climb up the shrubbery. But as he walks over to a lowered section, he spots a gate to his right. He walks towards it, barefoot, while tossing a mint from his pocket into his mouth.

Once inside the gate Walter is faced with a large pond, circled by a crushed gravel pathway. He is struggling to see very far through the thick haze that is hovering above the pond, like steam coming off a hot spring. He begins to worry that the football may have landed in the water, when he suddenly spots a flash of green on the edge of the pathway beside the pond. He makes his way over and as he gets closer he can

see that the 'green' is moving, zigzagging in jolty movements. It is not the football after all, but something much smaller — an emerald green dragonfly, twisting and turning as it darts between the water and land.

And suddenly, Walter's attention is captured by an item soaring towards him. It's a straw hat, bouncing along in the wind. Its flight is abruptly cut short as it gets hooked by the end of a gum tree's branch, a few metres from where Walter is standing. Walter walks over and stretches his arm high. He unhooks the hat off the sharp branch, just as he sees a woman, hatless, bounding towards him. He hands the hat over to the woman. She smiles and thanks him for his help. He feels something shift in his body; his chest feels lighter.

The woman keeps walking down the path. Walter turns around and steps towards the edge of the pond. He crouches down in the grass and leans forward to look deeper into the water, searching for the football.

The dragonfly whizzes out in front of him. It then lands on the back of Walter's left hand. He gasps. He has never had a dragonfly land on him before. He knows how rare it is. He holds his hand still, trying not to startle it as the fluttering of its wings slows down.

Walter stares at the intriguing insect. He notices its dominating and bulging eyes, wide-stretched wings and the tiny hairs on its body. Something feels very familiar about this elaborate insect. And then he realizes: here is a miniature, much less frightening version of the giant flying insect on his game back home.

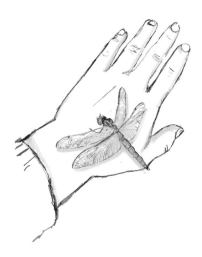

A sharp chattering sound, coming from above Walter's head, interrupts him. He looks above his head and sees a magpie perched on one of the gum tree's high branches. Its squawking intermingles with the rustle of the gum leaves. Walter looks all around him: the dragonfly, the caw and the whispering trees …

It's all here, he realizes.

He thinks about the virtual world behind his screen at home, how much it resembles here. *Or does here resemble the game?* he questions, as though he has lost track of what is mimicking what.

He looks at his surroundings, all that is around him, as though he is seeing it for the first time. Suddenly, he feels like he can focus properly — similar to what he experiences when he is conquering an algorithmic enemy or absorbed in scrolling through the portal of infinite information available in the palm of his hand. But there's another feeling that's also there. A feeling of ease.

Just from noticing a dragonfly, magpie and tree? he questions. *Without a quest to master or a finale to strive for?*

And so, Walter explores further. He doesn't just hear the magpie caw and leaves rustle … he listens.

He doesn't just see the dragonfly's elaborate body … he watches.

He doesn't just smell the scent of the eucalyptus leaves … he inhales.

He doesn't just touch the moist grass under his feet … he feels.

He doesn't just taste the spearmint in his mouth … he savours.

'Wow,' he exclaims out aloud, in awe. Walter's newfound calmness now also feels intensely alive.

Walter gazes down at the dragonfly more closely. He looks at the diaphanous wings, paper thin and wafery. The iridescent green on its back is shimmering brightly before his eyes. He feels the gentle pinpricks of the dragonfly's tiny feet on his skin. So much detail and sophistication on this small body of nature. The dragonfly's wafery wings start buzzing and it takes flight again, fluttering away.

The dragonfly scurries away from the pond and into the sight of another admirer — a young child who is being pushed in a stroller along the gravel path. Walter watches as the child's eyes, transfixed with wonder, intensely follow the dragonfly's dynamic acrobatics. The child then starts giggling at the dragonfly's imperfect movements, its sharp and unpredictable changes in direction, as though it's perpetually changing its mind about which way to fly.

Hmm … perhaps here is not so like the game after all.

Walter begins to stand up, his legs now feeling lighter above his grounded bare feet. He looks around further.

The haze has begun to lift.

Walter suddenly spots the green football lying in a small shrub a few metres from the tree. He runs to pick it up and then races away from the pond and bounds back through the gate.

He reaches the grassed area.

'Here, catch!' he yells at his friends, as his foot makes loud contact with the ball.

The ball soars into the air and straight into the hands of one of his friends. Walter punches the air and runs over to them, collecting his shoes on the way. The three friends then continue walking through the park, laughing as they dodge the puddles of rain.

The next morning, Walter wakes early after a deep sleep following the long afternoon at the park. He is about to leave for the bus stop, but first walks into the living room to look for his blue cap. He moves to flick the lights on, this time focusing on the switch as he does. The lights turn on.

He spots the blue cap sitting on the end of the couch. He runs over to grab it before turning the lights off again, and dashes to the front door.

As Walter is walking down the street, his phone pings. His stomach does an automatic backflip in tandem with the popped-up memory of the past days of gruelling waiting.

He sees an alert for a new email. He taps the rectangle box, just as he's interrupted.

'Good morning, lad.' Walter looks up to see an older man standing behind a short picket fence, watering a hedge of jasmine.

'Morning,' Walter smiles back.

This time Walter dodges the jasmine bush just as a dragonfly whizzes out — this one with a cheery red body — and starts hovering over the spray of his neighbour's hose. Walter's eyes follow the dragonfly's flight for a few moments. He then puts his phone in his right pocket and inhales the sweet scent of jasmine as he keeps walking.

Walter arrives at the bus stop and sits down on the bench. He leans forward slightly to look down the street for the bus. Not yet. He settles in more comfortably on the bench seat, ready to wait. He takes a deep breath as he notices the urge to reach into his right pocket. Instead, he turns his gaze and notices a woman wearing a hooded jacket sitting next to him. She looks familiar, but he is unsure why. The woman is looking back at Walter. She smiles, shyly. And they begin talking.

Afterword

Disconnection from the physical world

We are born into the world with an instinct to be present. As infants, we watch the world around us attentively, with curiosity and wonder, as we discover the world for the first time.

As we get older and come to know the world, we forget that it is enigmatic and mysterious. We begin to lose our sense of wonder with our surroundings. And this happens at the same time we learn to think. We then begin to experience the world through thought.

As adults, our minds are in a constant stream of thought. Most of this thinking happens beyond our conscious control and is motivated by survival; a lot of our thinking is underpinned by the mind's innate drive to avoid pain and seek pleasure, which functions to protect our safety and to ensure the continuation of our species.

Our minds regularly take us into the past and future. We often ruminate about the past or worry about the future, which is essentially the mind trying to find control and to avoid discomfort in order to feel safe.

Sometimes our mind will take us into the future to deliberately retreat from the present moment. This occurs when we want something to be over, or when we want something more appealing to begin. When this happens, we tend to avoid living fully and doing what matters until we reach the future desired moment. And when we get there, our minds will typically find something else in the future to jump to. Consequently, we end up spending a lot of time in our 'heads' rather than connected to the present moment.

In addition to the screen of our thinking, our modern-day society is now also challenged by another type of screen: digital screens. Our engagement with, and growing dependence on, the genius of the digital world (including the virtual world) has added another layer of disconnection. Like a moth to a flame, our hardwired instinct to avoid pain and seek pleasure draws us to the digital world's guarantee of quick distraction and alluring escapism. Even just seeing one notification of a new email or someone 'liking' our social media post results in a dopamine hit — the 'feel good' hormone that our brains are wired to seek. We are therefore becoming increasingly addicted to the boundless information and activity that is easily accessed through the device in our hands, screening us off from the physical world in front of us — including other people.

We are becoming increasingly disconnected from each other. And this goes against the core substance of being human. As with most primates, we are innately social; being part of a community, including sharing resources and collectively experiencing daily life, helped our ancestors to survive in the wild. We are therefore wired to seek togetherness and belonging. But the technological advances of modern-day times, including the accelerated emergence of artificial intelligence, is creating a more individualistic society. We rely on each other less. We trust each other less. And this is deeply inhibiting our ability to be fully present and weakening how much we value and prioritize human connection.

The consequences of disconnection

Losing connection with the present moment can therefore hurt us in two predominant ways.

First, when the location of our distracted attention triggers emotional distress, for example, when our mind engages in automatic thinking styles — such as worry, rumination, assumption making, catastrophizing etc. — featuring content that is not helping us. Another example is when our attention is caught up in unhelpful content and information in the digital world, including the abundance of unregulated material and disinhibited interpersonal behaviour that can be harmful to our mental health.

Second, when we miss out on the integral value and meaning that comes from being wondrous and curious about our physical world.

The importance of wonder and connection to the world

We do not experience our physical world fully unless we choose to bring our attention to our surroundings. This experience can be remarkably enhanced by reigniting our sense of wonder.

A sense of wonder allows us to be 'wowed' by the mystery and beauty in all that miraculously exists in the physical world. In particular, the natural world — which includes the existence of all human beings.

Choosing to reclaim a sense of wonder about our physical world can have a positive 'unselfing' impact on us. By connecting to the vastness and mystery of the world around us, we are more likely to step out of our ego — the mental stories and chatter that we have about ourselves — and see beyond our worries. And beyond ourselves. We can then realize that our purpose is simply being a human being, together with other human beings, in this grand and enigmatic natural world.

As described by pioneering conservationist Rachel Carson in her essay *The Sense of Wonder*:

> Those who dwell among the beauties and mysteries of the Earth are never alone or weary of life … Those who contemplate the beauty of the Earth find reserves of strength that will endure as long as life lasts.

And we can live this way of being with the world in small ways, every single day. It can be as simple as looking up at the ever-changing pattern of clouds; or smelling the crisp winter air; or noticing the enchanting hundred-year-old trees lining our streets; or lifting our heads up to smile at the stranger walking past us on the footpath. The humble, but elaborate physical world around us. That is always there.

Turning the lights on

Being connected to the world, with wonder, is not difficult. Our adult minds are just not very good at doing it, particularly when our thought screens and digital screens unknowingly hijack our attention.

A helpful way to think about being connected is to liken the experience to a light switch. We don't need the lights on all the time. Just as we don't need to be connected to the physical world all the time. But rather, it is helpful to notice when our attention has become switched off, and when being in the dark or haze — being disconnected from the world — is not helping us. In that case, we can then *choose* to switch the lights back on; choose to 'turn on' our wonder and connection to world. Through our senses.

From senses to 'sensing'

Our senses are always operating at the physical level — our body automatically sees, hears, touches, smells and tastes through its biological faculties. However, if our attention is not switched on to our senses, we don't fully sense the world. It is therefore helpful to turn our sensing into a verb — to actively engage with our senses. Attentionally, and intentionally.

Additionally, we can sprinkle in a sense of wonder to our sensing by adding a 'wow', as though we are experiencing the moment for the first time. This is what is often referred to as 'the beginner's mind' (a term and concept that comes from Zen Buddhism). Adding a 'wow' to our sensing allows us to elevate our ordinary moments to something extraordinary. Just like Walter we can …

Not just see, but watch.

Not just hear, but listen.

Not just touch, but feel.

Not just smell, but inhale.

Not just taste, but savour.

And bring a 'wow' of wonder and curiosity to that experience.

In summary

Choosing to be more present and connected to the physical world, including our fellow humans, has two powerful benefits. First, it helps to minimize the negative impact of our thoughts and digital screens. Second, it enhances our ordinary moments, where disconnect is stopping these moments from being extraordinary.

There is so much beauty in the physical world. Around us. All the time. But just because beauty exists in our world, does not mean it exists in our lives. We only experience it in our lives, in our beingness, if we intentionally choose to attend to it. Not for any particular quest or destination, but rather to master the art of being in this hard, yet wondrous, world.

The Being Human method

The Being Human method brings together each process presented in the four books of the Being Human series. It is a method that involves four steps for awareness and connection. The first two steps — 'hello mind' and 'hello heart' — allow us to be aware of our humanness. The second two steps — 'hello being' and 'hello world' — allow us to connect to our beingness with ourselves, our fellow humans and the physical world.

You can practise just one step or the full method, in any moment. It is particularly helpful when you are experiencing psychological distress or unhelpful distraction/ disconnection.

1. Hello mind

a. Notice your thoughts — that is, what your mind is saying to you.

b. Identify whether these thoughts are a familiar 'story' that your mind has told you before. For example, your mind might be telling you thoughts around the 'I'm not good enough' story or the 'No one cares about me' story.

c. Ask yourself whether your thoughts are helping you right now.

'Hello mind. These thoughts are an old story.
They are not helping me right now.'

2. Hello heart

a. Name the feeling/sensations in your body.

b. Identify the value underneath the feeling — what is it that matters to you for this feeling to be there?

c. Allow the feeling/sensations to be there (without judging yourself or the feeling).

It can help to ground yourself by placing a hand on your heart and taking a slow, deep breath as you gently say to yourself:

> *'Hello heart. I am feeling [...]*
> *because I care about [value].*
> *And that's okay.'*

And now that you are connected to your values …

3. Hello being

Say hello to who you want to be in the world.

   a. Check in with your values (i.e. the person you want to be) in that moment.

   b. Choose a response/behaviour in alignment with your values.

Gently say to yourself:

> *'Hello being. Who do I want to be in the world right now?'*

4. Hello world

Say hello to the world around you. Reconnect to the physical world, including nature and people around you, by connecting with your senses.

Don't just see, but watch.

Don't just hear, but listen.

Don't just touch, but feel.

Don't just smell, but inhale.

Don't just taste, but savour.

And where appropriate, bring a 'wow' to that experience.

'Hello mind. Hello heart.
Hello being. Hello world.'

Resources

General resources

Baird, J. 2020, *Phosphorescence: On awe, wonder and things that sustain you when the world goes dark*, 4th Estate.

Brown, B. 2021, *Daring Greatly: How the courage to be vulnerable transforms the way we live, love, parent, and lead*, Penguin Life.

Carlson, R. 2017, *The Sense of Wonder: A celebration of nature for parents and children*, HarperCollins Publishers.

Coates, K. and Kolkka, S. 2022, *How to Be Well: A handbook for women*, Simon & Schuster.

Goodwin, K. 2023, *Dear Digital, We Need to Talk: A guilt-free guide to taming your tech habits and thriving in a distracted world*, Major Street Publishing.

Hari, J. 2022, *Stolen Focus: Why you can't pay attention*. Bloomsbury.

Johnson, S. 1999, *Who Moved My Cheese? An amazing way to deal with work and your life*, Vermilion.

Katie, B. 2018, *A Mind at Home with Itself: How asking four questions can free your mind, open your heart, and turn your world*, HarperOne.

Siegel, D. J. 2016, *Mind: A journey to the heart of being human*, W.W. Norton & Company.

Siegel, D, J. 2012, *Mindsight: The new science of personal transformation*, Bantam Books.

ACT resources

Eifert, G.H., McKay, M. and Forsyth, J.P. 2006, *ACT on Life Not on Anger: The new Acceptance & Commitment Therapy guide to problem anger*, New Harbinger Publications.

Harris, R. 2016, *The Single Most Powerful Technique for Extreme Fusion*, e-book, www.actmindfully.com.au/ upimages/The_Single_Most_Powerful_Technique_for_Extreme_Fusion_-_Russ_Harris_-_October_2016.pdf

Harris, R. 2021, *The Happiness Trap: Stop struggling, start living*, 2nd edition. Exisle Publishing.

Hayes, L.L., Ciarrochi, J.V. and Bailey, A. 2022, *What Makes You Stronger: How to thrive in the face of change and uncertainty using Acceptance and Commitment Therapy*, New Harbinger.

Hayes, S. 2019, *A Liberated Mind: How to pivot toward what matters*, Avery.

Hayes, S.C. and Smith, S. 2005, *Get Out of Your Mind and Into Your Life: The new Acceptance and Commitment Therapy*, New Harbinger.

Leonard-Curtain, A. and Leonard-Curtain, T. 2019, *The power of small: How to make tiny but powerful changes when everything feels too much*, Hachette.

LeJeune, J. 'Pain and value: Two sides of the same coin', https://portlandpsychotherapy.com/2012/06/pain-and-values-two-sides-same-coin-0/

Oliver, J., Hill, J. and Morris, E. 2015, *Activate Your Life: Using acceptance and mindfulness to build a life that is rich, fulfilling and fun*, Constable & Robinson.

Acknowledgments

A heartfelt thank you to the team at Exisle Publishing for giving these books a welcoming home. A particular thank you to Gareth for seeing the potential in this series and to Anouska, Karen and Enni for taking such good care of these stories.

To the very talented Lizzie Szekely — I adore working with you and am constantly dazzled by your creative mind and your beautiful illustrations. Thank you for being so dedicated to these books and for befriending the 'W' characters the way you have.

I would like to thank Virginia Lloyd for her brilliance in editing the earlier versions of this series, and for her overall support in shaping this vision.

There were a number of friends and colleagues who generously gave their time to read initial manuscripts in this series and give their feedback: Kate James, Russ Harris,

Aisling Curtain, Louise Hayes. I would also like to thank other folk within the ACBS community, for introducing me to ACT and for creating such a supportive community.

I am hugely grateful for my friends and family:

Warwick — for being a loyal cheerleader of this series. And of us.

Amber and Trinity — for your enthusiasm and support.

Ryan — for the time, care and wisdom you have given this series. Your way with the written word blows my mind.

My parents — Mum, Andrew, Dad and Chrissi — for your endless love, support, and for your devotion to your grandchildren.

Spencer, Alfie and Sullivan — you are my best little teachers of being attentive, curious and playful.

Thank you to all the human beings who have joined me in my therapy room — thank you for trusting me. Thank you for teaching me.

And finally, thank you to everyone who stepped into the first version of Winnie's world, and to those embarking on this Being Human series. I hope that reading the characters' stories helps you to normalise and choose compassion for our complex humanness, and to revel in our extraordinary world.

It really is so rare and beautiful that we even exist.